D1189352

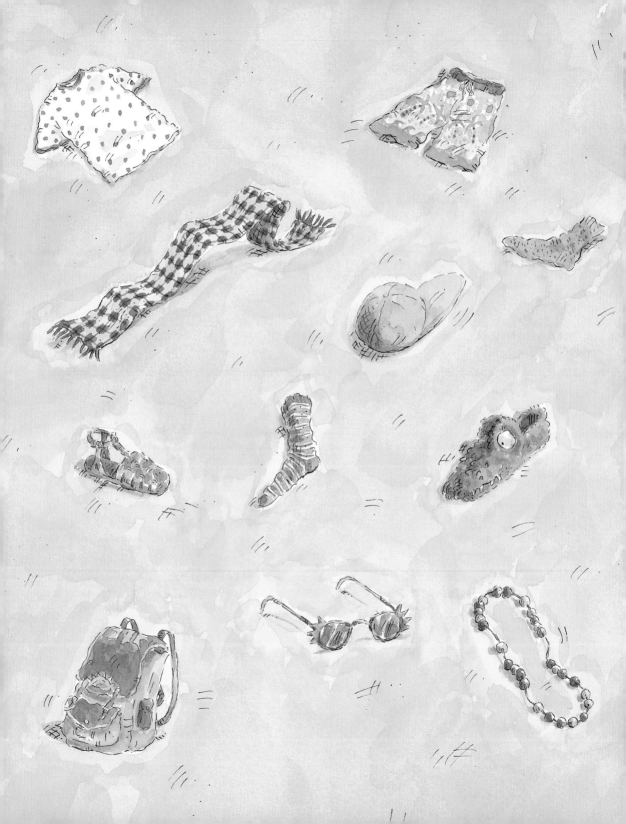

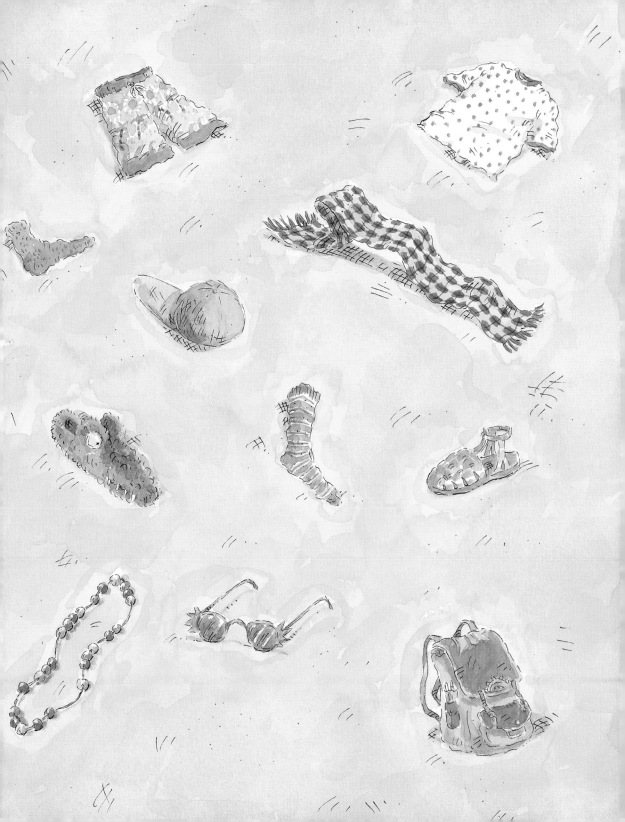

To parents and teachers

We hope you and the children will enjoy reading this story in either English or French. The story is simple, but not *simplified* so the language of the French and the English is quite natural but there is lots of repetition.

At the back of the book is a small picture dictionary with the key words and how to pronounce them. There is also a simple pronunciation guide to the whole story on the last page.

Here are a few suggestions on using the book:

• Read the story aloud in English first, to get to know it. Treat it like any other picture book: look at the pictures, talk about the story and the characters and so on.

• Then look at the picture dictionary and say the French names for the key words. Ask the children to repeat them. Concentrate on speaking the words out loud, rather than reading them.

• Go back and read the story again, this time in English *and* French. Don't worry if your pronunciation isn't quite correct. Just have fun trying it out. Check the guide at the back of the book, if necessary, but you'll soon pick up how to say the French words.

• When you think you and the children are ready, you can try reading the story in French only. Ask the children to say it with you. Only ask them to read it if they are keen to try. The spelling could be confusing and put them off.

• Above all encourage the children to have a go and give lots of praise. Little children are usually quite unselfconscious and this is excellent for building up confidence in a foreign language.

Published by b small publishing ltd.
The Book Shed, 36 Leyborne Park, Kew, Richmond, Surrey, TW9 3HA, UK
www.bsmall.co.uk   www.facebook.com/bsmallpublishing   @bsmallbear
© b small publishing ltd., 1998. This new edition published 2012
1 2 3 4 5
All rights reserved.
Design: *Lone Morton and Louise Millar*   Editorial: *Catherine Bruzzone and Susan Martineau*
Production: *Madeleine Ehm*
Colour reproduction: *Vimnice Printing Press Co. Ltd.* Printed in China by *WKT Co. Ltd.*
ISBN: 978-1-905710-02-7
British Library Cataloguing in Publication Data. A catalogue record for this book is available from the British Library.

Get dressed, Robbie

Habille-toi, Robbie

Lone Morton

Pictures by Anna C. Leplar
French by Christophe Dillinger

b small publishing

Every morning, Robbie's mum lays out clothes for him to get dressed.

Chaque matin, la maman de Robbie lui prépare des habits pour qu'il s'habille.

But some mornings Robbie likes to choose his own clothes.

Mais certains matins, Robbie préfère choisir ses habits tout seul.

Sometimes Robbie puts on clothes that are too big,

Parfois Robbie met des habits qui sont trop grands,

sometimes clothes that are too small.

parfois des habits qui sont trop petits.

Sometimes Robbie puts on winter clothes,

Parfois Robbie met des habits d'hiver,

sometimes summer clothes.

parfois des habits d'été.

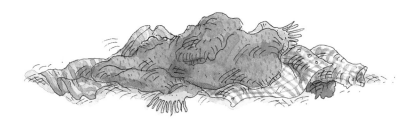

And sometimes he puts on clothes
from his dressing-up box!

Et parfois il choisit des habits dans
sa malle à déguisements!

But today, Robbie puts on his green, spotty T-shirt,

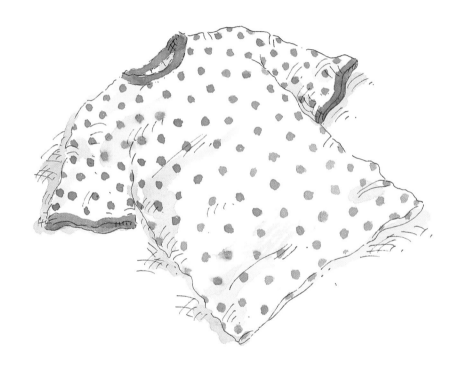

Mais aujourd'hui, Robbie choisit son T-shirt vert à pois,

his patterned shorts,

son short à motifs,

one orange sock,
une chaussette orange,

one stripey sock,
une chaussette à rayures,

one blue plastic sandal,
une sandale en plastique bleu,

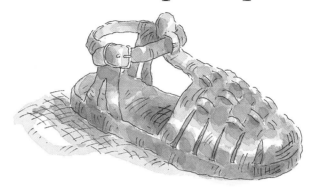

one crocodile slipper,
un chausson en forme de crocodile,

his pink baseball cap,
sa casquette de baseball rose,

a very long, checked scarf,
une très longue écharpe à carreaux,

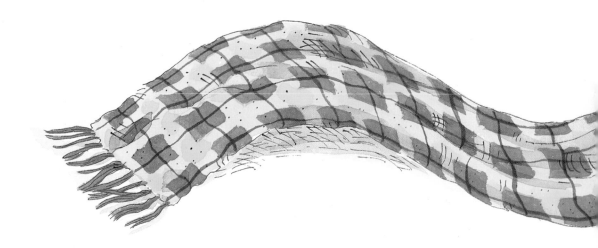

a pair of sunglasses,
une paire de lunettes de soleil,

a necklace of wooden beads,
un collier de boules en bois,

and his brand-new rucksack with his favourite car and ten coloured crayons.

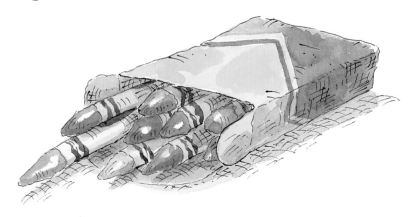

et son sac à dos tout neuf avec sa voiture préférée et dix crayons de couleur.

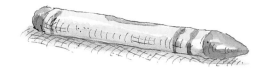

"Robbie, we've got to go out!"
calls Mum. "Are you dressed yet?"

"Robbie, il est l'heure de sortir!"
crie maman. "Es-tu enfin habillé?"

"Yes," says Robbie. "I am dressed.

I'm going to wear this…!"

"Oui," dit Robbie. "Je suis habillé.

Je vais mettre ça…!"

Pronouncing French

Don't worry if your pronunciation isn't quite correct. The important thing is to be willing to try. The pronunciation guide here will help but it cannot be completely accurate:

• Read the guide as naturally as possible, as if it were British English.

• Put stress on the letters in *italics,* e.g. show-*set*

• Don't roll the r at the end of the word, for example in the French word **le** (the): ler.

If you can, ask a French person to help and move on as soon as possible to speaking the words without the guide.

Note French adjectives usually have two forms, one for masculine and one for feminine nouns. They often look very similar but are pronounced slightly differently, e.g. **petit** and **petite** (see below).

Words Les Mots

leh moh

clothes
les habits

lez *abee*

T-shirt
le T-shirt

ler tee-*shirt*

big
grand/grande

groh/grond

small
petit/petite

p'*tee*/p'*teet*

shorts
le short
ler short

sandals
les sandales
leh sondal

scarf
l'écharpe
lehsharp

socks
les chaussettes
leh show-set

rucksack
le sac à dos
ler sak ah doh

slipper
le chausson
ler showss-oh

sunglasses
les lunettes de soleil
leh loonet der solay

car
la voiture
lah vwat-yoor

green
vert/verte
vair/vairt

orange
orange
o-*ronsh*

blue
bleu/bleue
bl'/bl'

pink
rose
roz

crayons
les crayons
leh cray*oh*

necklace
le collier
ler colee-*eh*

winter
l'hiver
lee*vair*

cap
la casquette
la kas-*ket*

summer
l'été
let-*ay*

stripey
à rayures
ah ray-*oor*

spotty
à pois
ah pwah

checked
à carreaux
ah kar*oh*

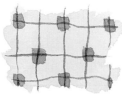

patterned
à motifs
ah mot*eef*

A simple guide to pronouncing this French story

Habille-toi, Robbie
a*bee* twah, ro*bee*

Chaque matin, la maman de Robbie lui prépare des habits
shack ma*tah*, la mam*oh* de ro*bee* lwee preh-*pah* deza*bee*

pour qu'il s'habille.
poor keel sa*bee*

Mais certains matins, Robbie préfère choisir ses habits tout seul.
meh sair*tah* ma*tah*, ro*bee* preh-*fair* shwah-*zeer* seza*bee* too sirl

Parfois Robbie met des habits qui sont trop grands,
pah-*fwah* ro*bee* meh deza*bee* kee soh troh groh

parfois des habits qui sont trop petits.
pah-*fwah* deza*bee* kee soh troh p'*tee*

Parfois Robbie met des habits d'hiver,
pah-*fwah* ro*bee* meh deza*bee* dee*vair*

parfois des habits d'été.
pah-*fwah* deza*bee* det-*ay*

Et parfois il choisit des habits dans sa malle à déguisements!
eh pah-*fwah* eel shwa*zee* deza*bee* doh sah mal ah deh-geez-*moh*

Mais aujourd'hui, Robbie choisit son T-shirt vert à pois,
meh o'shoor-*dwee*, ro*bee* shwa*zee* soh tee-*shirt* vair ah pwah

son short à motifs,
soh short ah mo*teef*

une chaussette orange
oon show-*set* o-*ronsh*

une chaussette à rayures,
oon show-*set* ah ray-*oor*

une sandale en plastique bleu,
oon son*dal* ohn plas*teek* bl'

un chausson en forme de crocodile,
ahn showss-*oh* ohn form der croko*deel*

sa casquette de baseball rose,
sah kas-*ket* der base*boll* roz

une très longue écharpe à carreaux,
oon treh longer eh*sharp* ah ka*roh*

une paire de lunettes de soleil,
oon pair der loo*net* der so*lay*

un collier de boules en bois,
ahn colee-*yeh* der bool ohn bwah

et son sac à dos tout neuf avec sa voiture préférée et dix crayons de couleur.
eh soh sak ah *doh* too nerf avek sa vwat-*yoor* prefair*ay* et dee cray*oh* der cooler

"Robbie, il est l'heure de sortir!" crie maman. "Es-tu enfin habillé?"
ro*bee*, eel eh lur der sor*teer*, cree ma*moh*, eh too oh*fah* abee*yeh*

"Oui," dit Robbie. "Je suis habillé. Je vais mettre ça...!"
wee, dee ro*bee*, sh' swee abee*yeh*, sh' veh mair-tr' sah